Contents

📕 TEACHER GUIDE
- Assessment Rubric **4**
- How Is This Literature Kit™ Organized? **5**
- Graphic Organizers **6**
- Bloom's Taxonomy for Reading Comprehension **7**
- Teaching Strategies **7**
- Summary of the Story **8**
- Vocabulary **9**

✏️ STUDENT HANDOUTS
- Spotlight on Anna Sewell **10**
- Chapter Questions
  - *Chapters 1 – 5* **11**
  - *Chapters 6 – 10* **14**
  - *Chapters 11 – 15* **17**
  - *Chapters 16 – 20* **20**
  - *Chapters 21 – 25* **23**
  - *Chapters 26 – 30* **26**
  - *Chapters 31 – 35* **29**
  - *Chapters 36 – 40* **32**
  - *Chapters 41 – 45* **35**
  - *Chapters 46 – 49* **38**
- Writing Tasks **41**
- Word Search **44**
- Comprehension Quiz **45**

EZ✓ EASY MARKING™ ANSWER KEY **47**

GRAPHIC ORGANIZERS **53**

✔ **6 BONUS Activity Pages!** Additional worksheets for your students **FREE!**

- Go to our website: **www.classroomcompletepress.com/bonus**
- Enter item CC2500 or Black Beauty
- Enter pass code CC2500D for Activity Pages

Assessment Rubric

Black Beauty

Student's Name: _____ Assignment: _____ Level: _____

	Level 1	Level 2	Level 3	Level 4
Comprehension of the Novel	Demonstrates a limited understanding of the novel	Demonstrates a basic understanding of the novel	Demonstrates a good understanding of the novel	Demonstrates a thorough understanding of the novel
Content	Information incomplete; key details missing	Some information complete; details missing	All required information complete; key details contain some description	All required information complete; enough description for clarity
Style	Little variety in word choice; language vague and imprecise	Some variety in word choice; language somewhat vague and imprecise	Good variety in word choice; language precise and quite descriptive	Writer's voice is apparent throughout. Excellent choice of words; precise language.
Conventions	Errors seriously interfere with the writer's purpose	Repeated errors in mechanics and usage	Some errors in convention	Few errors in convention

STRENGTHS:

WEAKNESSES:

NEXT STEPS:

Before You Teach

Teacher Guide

*This resource has been created for ease of use by both **TEACHERS** and **STUDENTS** alike.*

Introduction

nna Sewell's novel, *Black Beauty*, is one of the most endearing stories of all time. An easy-to-read classic, it is set in mid-Nineteenth Century England and is told from the perspective of the horse, Black Beauty. Over the course of the novel, Black Beauty has numerous adventures with a host of characters, both human and animal. Many of his adventures, however, are marked by tragedy. Through it all, the reader gains a fascinating glimpse into the Nineteenth Century world of England, and is able to identify and appreciate many of the injustices experienced by not only the horses of the day, but society's poor and downtrodden as well.

How Is Our Literature Kit™ Organized?

STUDENT HANDOUTS

Chapter Activities *(in the form of reproducible worksheets)* make up the majority of our resource. For each chapter or group of chapters there are BEFORE YOU READ activities and AFTER YOU READ activities.

- The BEFORE YOU READ activities prepare students for reading by setting a purpose for reading. They stimulate background knowledge and experience, and guide students to make connections between what they know and what they will learn. Important concepts and vocabulary from the chapter(s) are also presented.

- The AFTER YOU READ activities check students' comprehension and extend their learning. Students are asked to give thoughtful consideration of the text through creative and evaluative short-answer questions and journal prompts.

Six **Writing Tasks** and three **Graphic Organizers** are included to further develop students' critical thinking and writing skills, and analysis of the text. *(See page 6 for suggestions on using the Graphic Organizers.)* The **Assessment Rubric** *(page 4)* is a useful tool for evaluating students' responses to the Writing Tasks and Graphic Organizers.

PICTURE CUES
Our resource contains three main types of pages, each with a different purpose and use. A **Picture Cue** at the top of each page shows, at a glance, what the page is for.

 Teacher Guide
- Information and tools for the teacher

 Student Handout
- Reproducible worksheets and activities

 Easy Marking™ Answer Key
- Answers for student activities

EASY MARKING™ ANSWER KEY
Marking students' worksheets is fast and easy with our **Answer Key**. Answers are listed in columns – just line up the column with its corresponding worksheet, as shown, and see how every question matches up with its answer!

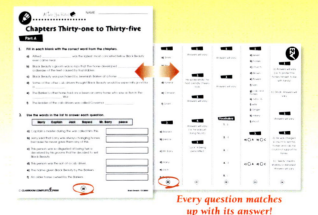

Every question matches up with its answer!

Before You Teach

1, 2, 3 Graphic Organizers

The three **Graphic Organizers** included in this Literature Kit™ are especially suited to a study of **Black Beauty**. Below are suggestions for using each organizer in your classroom, or they may be adapted to suit the individual needs of your students. The organizers can be used on a projection system or interactive whiteboard in teacher-led activities, and/or photocopied for use as student worksheets. To evaluate students' responses to any of the organizers, you may wish to use the **Assessment Rubric** (on page 4).

OWNERS, OWNERS EVERYWHERE

In writing *Black Beauty*, Anna Sewell effectively brought to light a key issue of her day – the inhumane treatment of horses by their owners. Sewell was able to convey this issue by creating a variety of characters who owned Black Beauty during his lifetime. Some of these owners were good and kind, while others were heartless and cruel. Still others meant well, but through their ignorance made Black Beauty's life very difficult. This Graphic Organizer asks students to recall Black Beauty's ten different owners and grooms (for those that are given) in chronological order, and evaluate whether each owner's treatment of Black Beauty was good, bad or so-so. **Found on Page 53.**

CONCEPT WHEEL

Black Beauty leads a very eventful life, and like a person, he experiences his share of joys and heartaches. Certainly many of his adventures make for very interesting reading. The Concept Wheel is an excellent tool to help students analyze story elements as they relate to a major event in the novel. Students are asked to choose one major event (for example, the death of Reuben Smith when he rode Black Beauty late one night while he was drunk) and provide details regarding the five Ws: what happened, who was there, when it happened, where it happened, and why it happened. **Found on Page 54.**

COMPARE AND CONTRAST MATRIX

Black Beauty features an array of fascinating characters, from the quiet and principled Jerry Barker, to the desperate Seedy Sam, to the greedy and thoughtless Nicholas Skinner. Even the horses that Black Beauty meets have very distinct personalities, including the quick-tempered Ginger and the fun-loving Merrylegs. Often, too, the author gives clues about a character by the name each is given. For this activity students are to choose either two human characters or two horses from the novel and compare three attributes of each. At least two of the attributes must pertain to personality or character. The third can be either a personality or physical attribute. **Found on Page 55.**

Bloom's Taxonomy* for Reading Comprehension

The activities in our resource engage and build the full range of thinking skills that are essential for students' reading comprehension. Based on the six levels of thinking in Bloom's Taxonomy, questions are given that challenge students to not only recall what they have read, but move beyond this to understand the text through higher-order thinking. By using higher-order skills of application, analysis, synthesis and evaluation, students become active readers, drawing more meaning from the text, and applying and extending their learning in more sophisticated ways.

Our **Literature Kit**, therefore, is an effective tool for any Language Arts program. Whether it is used in whole or in part, or adapted to meet individual student needs, our resource provides teachers with the important questions to ask, inspiring students' interest, creativity, and promoting meaningful learning.

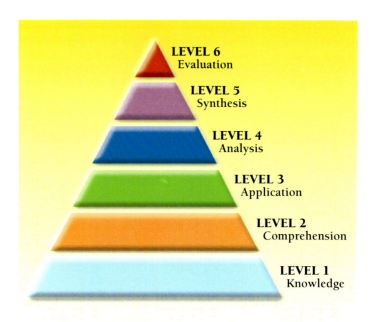

BLOOM'S TAXONOMY: 6 LEVELS OF THINKING

*Bloom's Taxonomy is a widely used tool by educators for classifying learning objectives, and is based on the work of Benjamin Bloom.

Teaching Strategies — WHOLE-CLASS, SMALL GROUP AND INDEPENDENT STUDY

Black Beauty is a novel that may be approached in several ways. Most obvious is as a traditional, whole-class read-aloud in which the teacher reads the book out loud to the entire class, stopping after one or more chapters for the students to answer the chapter questions. As they complete the questions, students reread the chapter(s) on their own. Depending on the interests and needs of your students, you may choose to apply some shared or modeled reading, focusing discussion on the author's skills, choices made in writing, and the elements of the narrative. The BEFORE YOU READ and AFTER YOU READ activities in this **Literature Kit** provide a basis for such discussions.

To facilitate small group and independent study learning, these activities have been divided into chapter groupings to allow students to work on manageable sections of the novel, and not feel overwhelmed by the activities. Teachers may also choose to use only a selection of the activities in this resource for small group or independent study, assigning tasks that match students' specific needs, and allowing students to work at their own speed. The components of this resource make it flexible and easy to adapt as not all of the activities need to be completed.

Teachers may wish to have their students keep a daily reading log so that they might record their daily progress and reflections. Journaling prompts have been included at the end of each chapter section to facilitate students' thinking and writing.

Summary of the Story

NOTHING can defeat the spirit of this gentle and courageous horse, Black Beauty.

Anna Sewell's novel, **Black Beauty**, is one of the most endearing stories of all time. It is set in England during the mid-1800's and is told from the perspective of its main character, the gentle horse, Black Beauty. Over the course of the novel, Black Beauty shares his life and adventures from his days as a young colt in the pastures of Farmer Grey, through a number of different owners and into his twilight years.

During Black Beauty's lifetime he is owned by several kind and thoughtful people, including Squire Gordon and Jerry Barker. However, he also comes into contact with other people who are cruel and thoughtless, like Nicholas Skinner and Reuben Smith.

Tragedy seems to shape the course of Black Beauty's life. One of his first owners, Squire Gordon, is forced to sell Black Beauty and all of his other horses when the Squire's wife becomes desperately ill. From then on, Black Beauty is passed from one owner to the next, and his circumstances and physical condition gradually deteriorate. Nothing, however, can defeat the spirit of this courageous animal. A pivotal incident in Black Beauty's life occurs when, despite having a broken shoe, he is driven hard by a drunken Reuben Smith. When Black Beauty stumbles, not only is his rider killed, but permanent damage is done to the horse's knees.

Black Beauty learns much of the world through the friendships he forms with many different horses: the tragic life of Ginger, the brave and noble Captain, and the fun-loving Merrylegs.

The reader also learns of the tremendous injustices which horses of the day were forced to endure, most especially the bearing rein – a device which forced the horse to have its head raised at all times, causing it much discomfort. This novel provides a fascinating glimpse of England during the Nineteenth Century, and gives readers a sense of the remarkable injustices experienced by both horses and people of the day.

Suggestions for Further Reading

Will James, **Smoky: The Cow Horse** © 1926
Enid Bagnold, **National Velvet** © 1935
Mary O'Hara, **My Friend Flicka** © 1940
Walter Farley, **The Black Stallion** © 1941
Marguerite Henry, **Misty of Chincoteague** © 1947
Marguerite Henry, **King of the Wind** © 1948
Marguerite Henry, **Stormy: Misty's Foal** © 1963
C.S. Lewis, **The Horse and His Boy** © 1954
Francis Kalnay, **Chucaro: Wild Pony of the Pampa** © 1958
Mari Sandoz, **The Horsecatcher** © 1962
Steven D. Price, **The Greatest Horse Stories Ever Told** © 2001

Vocabulary

CHAPTERS 1 TO 5
• canter • farrier • vice • crupper • roan • restive • paddock • astonish • shriek • halter • harness • chaise • breeching • skirted • blinkers • accustom • girths • pales • disregard • accommodation

CHAPTERS 6 TO 10
• discontented • fidget • pined • flanks • filly • obliged • hock • chafed • civil • warranted • indignity • disfigure • liberty • skittish • weaned • forelock • halter • sieve • flog • spurs

CHAPTERS 11 TO 15
• droll • livery • chaise • wrenched • hostler • oppressed • fatigued • haunches • brutal • passions • grieved • regiment • bayonet • lulled • prompt • furious • riles • obliged • aggravate

CHAPTERS 16 TO 20
• halters • smother • din • violently • mortal • heathenish • confidentially • mauled • roused • mistress • draught • ignorance • flogging • magistrate • interfere • impudent • squire • evidence • pined • twitch

CHAPTERS 21 TO 25
• peculiar • imperious • vexed • amiable • obliged • anxious • governess • situation • character • refreshment • constitution • peculiarities • irritable • accustomed • nuisance • respectfully • drab • constant • terret

CHAPTERS 26 TO 30
• slovenly • consequence • commotion • contempt • caustic • inquest • blemishes • conversation • foremost • sufficiently • inquest • warrant • tolerably • fatiguing • tormenting • phaeton • contemptuously • cob • cockney • dun

CHAPTERS 31 TO 35
• indolent • dejected • palisades • restive • sham • portmanteau • feverish • tow • dejected • monstrous • dumpling • crupper • snaffle • cantered • animated • piteous • beseeching • sham • jaded • omnibuses

CHAPTERS 36 TO 40
• foundling • convenient • thronged • oppressed • lank • oblige • shafts • bade • compliments • hawthorn • wrongdoer • abusive • mockery • delicate • fetlocks • knackers • sovereign • shilling • mackintoshes • doctrine

CHAPTERS 41 TO 45
• blackguards • pinafore • blemish • repent • exhausted • liable • accord • gentry • pluckiest • premises • bewildered • feeble • pining • consequence • stern • constitution • lunatic • asylum • vexation

CHAPTERS 46 TO 49
• frequently • persuasive • fatigue • detain • permanent • indignities • misery • beseech • cordial • sufficient • goad • venture • obliged • carter • purblind • niter • porter • injustice • linseed • caresses

Anna Sewell (1820 – 1878)

We call them dumb animals, and so they are, for they cannot tell us how they feel, but they do not suffer less because they have no words. (Anna Sewell)

Anna Sewell was born in Norfolk, England in 1820. At fourteen she was seriously injured when she was walking home from school in the rain – she fell and injured both her ankles. For the remainder of her life she had difficulty walking and standing. She therefore spent much of her life indoors or being drawn about the English countryside in horse-drawn carriages. Partially as a result of this she came to love horses and developed a great concern for the humane and healthy treatment of animals.

Sewell never married and lived at home for her entire life. Like the rest of her family, Anna was a Quaker, who was very active in helping those she came into contact with. Although **Black Beauty** was the only novel written by Sewell, her mother (Mary Wright Sewell) was a successful writer for children, so Anna became quite accomplished at editing her mother's texts and familiarizing herself with the writing process.

Anna wrote her novel, **Black Beauty**, between the years 1871 and 1877, a time in her life when her health was declining. Much of the text she dictated to her mother. When it was completed she sold the manuscript to local publishers for only 40 Pounds (approximately 70 U.S. Dollars). **Black Beauty** was published only five months before Sewell's death, and went on to become one of the endearing classics, beloved by children and adults alike for almost 150 years. Today it holds the distinction of being the sixth best seller in the English language!

Did You Know?

- Anna Sewell's birthplace in Church Plain, Great Yarmouth, England, is now a museum
- The bearing rein, which was very hard on horses, went out of style as a direct outcome of the novel's popularity
- The horse, Black Beauty, was actually based on a horse owned by Anna's brother, Phillip

NAME: _____

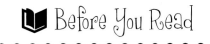

Chapters One to Five

Answer the questions in complete sentences.

1. Throughout history horses have been one of the most popular and useful animals to humankind. Describe a personal encounter that you have experienced with a horse. This may be a real experience with a real horse, or one you have enjoyed through the printed word – or even through another media (such as a movie or television program).

   _____
   _____

2. Research one of the following: an interesting quote about horses; the name of a really good book or movie about a horse; or a personal story or anecdote that a friend or family member told you which involves a horse.

   _____
   _____

Vocabulary

Complete each sentence with a word from the list.

| roan | canter | restive | farrier | crupper | paddock | vice |

1. The _____ was an expert at putting shoes on horses.

2. Black Beauty began to _____ happily down the lane.

3. The only _____ my grandmother would admit to was placing the odd bet at the local racetrack.

4. The leather _____ dangled dangerously from the horse's saddle.

5. The black stallion's mother was a beautiful chestnut _____.

6. After spending his third day in the stall, Merrylegs began getting quite _____.

7. The Squire's stable of horses loved to gallop around the large _____ which was located just behind the barn.

After You Read

NAME: _____

Chapters One to Five

Part A

Put a check mark next to the answer that is most correct.

1. **What words best describe Black Beauty's first owner?**
   - ○ A   cruel and thoughtless
   - ○ B   kind and considerate
   - ○ C   loud and boisterous
   - ○ D   absent-minded and neglectful

2. **What did Black Beauty's mother think of the sport of hunting hares?**
   - ○ A   It was a fascinating sport.
   - ○ B   She couldn't understand why it was so popular with men.
   - ○ C   She wished someone would invite her to join.
   - ○ D   She hoped that Black Beauty would one day join the hunt.

3. **As a part of Black Beauty's training the Squire sent him to a neighboring meadow which was close to a nearby:**
   - ○ A   airport
   - ○ B   busy highway
   - ○ C   railway
   - ○ D   canal

4. **What was the name of the horse that had the bad habit of biting and snapping?**
   - ○ A   Ginger
   - ○ B   Merrylegs
   - ○ C   Rob Roy
   - ○ D   Duchess

5. **Who was it that gave Black Beauty his name?**
   - ○ A   the Squire
   - ○ B   John Howard, the stable boy
   - ○ C   Black Beauty's mother
   - ○ D   the Squire's wife, Mrs. Gordon

NAME: _____

After You Read

Chapters One to Five

Part B

Answer the questions in complete sentences.

1. The **setting** of a story includes where and when the events take place. The first five chapters of this novel do not lend a great deal of detail as to the setting, but from the clues offered, where and when do you think the story is set?
   _____

2. Consider for a moment what it would be like to live the life of a horse. Why is the type of master who owns you very important as to the quality of life you might lead? Be sure to give details.
   _____
   _____

3. Why was the hare hunting incident in this section so tragic?
   _____

4. Why do you think Black Beauty's original master sold him to Squire Gordon? Why might such an event be difficult for a horse? (Try to think of two reasons.)
   _____
   _____

5. The same English word can often be used as either a **noun** or a **verb**, depending on how it is used in the sentence. One example from these chapters is "groom". As a noun it can mean "a person who looks after horses". As a verb it can mean "to make neat and trim". Another word used in this section that can be used as both a noun and verb is **skirt**. Use "skirt" in sentences showing the meanings of the word as both noun and verb.
   _____

You have just begun reading one of the most famous novels ever written. Give your impressions of the novel after five chapters. Tell briefly what has happened to this point, what you have enjoyed about the novel, and what you hope will happen in the coming chapters.

 NAME: _____

Chapters Six to Ten

Answer the questions in complete sentences.

1. Chapter Six is entitled, **Liberty**, and describes Black Beauty's yearning for more freedom in his life. Why do you think liberty is such an important thing in the life of a person – or a horse?
   _____
   _____

2. Investigate: In horseback riding, what was the purpose of the spur? How might a horse resent such an instrument?
   _____
   _____

Vocabulary

With a straight line, connect each word on the left with its meaning on the right.

1	discontented		sides	A
2	fidget		shame	B
3	pined		polite	C
4	flanks		deserved	D
5	filly		unhappy	E
6	obliged		rubbed	F
7	hock		yearned	G
8	chafed		forced	H
9	civil		a leg joint	I
10	warranted		scar	J
11	indignity		young female horse	K
12	disfigure		squirm	L

NAME: _____

After You Read

Chapters Six to Ten

Part A

1. **Circle T if the statement is TRUE or F if it is FALSE.**

   T   F   a) Ginger believed that if she had enjoyed the same upbringing as Black Beauty, her disposition would have been greatly improved.

   T   F   b) Even though a tail would have been useful for Sir Oliver to brush off the flies, he was still extremely proud to have had his tail docked.

   T   F   c) Ginger reacted in the same manner to people whether she was being treated cruelly or gently.

   T   F   d) Early in Ginger's life she came to believe that men were her natural enemies and she must defend herself.

   T   F   e) Black Beauty was always called upon for taking the children riding.

   T   F   f) When the family went out for a riding party, the four horses used were Black Beauty, Ginger, Sir Oliver and Merrylegs.

2. **Number the events from 1 to 6 in the order they occurred in the chapters.**

   _____ a) The horses discuss the evils of the practice of tail-docking.

   _____ b) Merrylegs teaches the boys a lesson.

   _____ c) Ginger tells of her dreadful experience with the bearing rein.

   _____ d) Black Beauty learns about the purpose of blinkers.

   _____ e) Ginger tells the story of her unfortunate encounter with Samson.

   _____ f) Black Beauty yearns for more liberty.

After You Read

NAME: _____

Chapters Six to Ten

Part B

Answer the questions in complete sentences.

1. If you were casting the roles in these chapters for a movie, what actors would you choose to play Mr. Ryder and Samson? Give an explanation for each of your choices.
   _____
   _____

2. What is meant by the expression "breaking a horse"?
   _____
   _____

3. Investigate: In Chapter Eight Ginger mentions the bearing rein and remarks on how dreadful it was. It was, in fact, because of this novel that the bearing rein fell into disuse in Great Britain. Find out how the bearing rein worked and why it was such a cruel instrument.
   _____
   _____

4. At one point in her story Ginger says, **"I was too high-mettled for that"**. How else might you describe Ginger's opinion of herself?
   _____

5. Compare the two different strategies suggested by Merrylegs and Ginger when dealing with the boys who used a riding stick on Merrylegs. Which strategy do you think would be more effective? Why?
   _____

In an earlier question you were asked to investigate the bearing rein. Now imagine for a moment that you are a horse who is being subjected to this cruel instrument. Write a description of exactly how it feels to be a horse whose master or mistress uses a bearing rein (both physically and emotionally).

NAME: _____

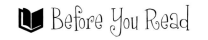

Chapters Eleven to Fifteen

1. The author, Anna Sewell writes, "... **if we see cruelty and wrong that we have the power to stop, and do nothing, we make ourselves sharers in the guilt**". Do you agree or disagree with this statement? Explain your reason.
   _____
   _____

2. In the time of Black Beauty, why was owning a horse more important for most people than it is today?
   _____
   _____

Vocabulary

Complete each sentence with a word from the list.

| droll | livery | chaise | wrenched | hostler | oppressed | fatigued |

1. When a horse is ill-treated, it will begin to feel _____.

2. The cruel boy _____ hard on the reins, jerking the pony's head backward.

3. Following the difficult journey through the mountains, the hiking party were badly _____.

4. Black Beauty was harnessed to a _____ for the trip into town.

5. The Squire had a very _____ sense of humor.

6. Ginger and Merrylegs were boarded in a _____ stable for the holidays.

7. The elderly _____ gave Black Beauty a rubdown in record time.

Chapters Eleven to Fifteen

Part A

1. Fill in each blank with the correct word from the chapters.

a) In Chapter Eleven, Black Beauty's master was upset by the way that _____ treated his horse.

b) Beauty probably saved his master's life by not crossing the _____ when it was not safe.

c) In the school and the playground _____ sons and laborers' sons were all alike.

d) James said that _____ **"was the devil's own trademark"**.

e) The master offered _____ the position of groom for his brother-in-law, Sir Clifford Williams.

f) Squire _____ was considered to be the best rider in the county.

Vocabulary

Use the words in the list to answer each question.

| Langley | John | Bushby | James | Grey |

a) The Squire worked for years with this Farmer in order to get the bearing reins done away with.

b) To whom did Mr. Gordon try to convince not to use the bearing reins?

c) Black Beauty, Mr. Gordon, and this man were caught in a violent storm.

d) What was the last name of the boy that was pitched over the head of his pony?

e) John gave a glowing character reference to the master about this person.

NAME: _____

After You Read

Chapters Eleven to Fifteen

Part B

Answer the questions in complete sentences.

1. Considering the events described thus far in the novel, describe what the following comment means: **"A man's life and a horse's life are worth more than a fox's tail."**
   _____
   _____

2. Why do you think the mistreatment of horses grieved Black Beauty's master so much?
   _____
   _____

3. Give one of the reasons that Mr. Gordon gave for not using the bearing reins in Chapter Eleven.
   _____
   _____

4. Give your opinion about the statement made in Chapter Thirteen, **"there is no religion without love"**. Do you agree or disagree? Defend your answer.
   _____
   _____

5. Put the following statement in your own words: **"By giving way to your passions you injure your own character as much, nay more, than you injure your horse."**
   _____
   _____

Most people at one time or another dream of owning a horse. If it were possible for you to own a horse, describe the horse that you would choose. Make sure to give as much detail as possible (for example, color, sex, name, size, its character, special abilities, etc.).

Before You Read

NAME: _____

Chapters Sixteen to Twenty

1. How does accepting one's responsibilities in a mature, competent manner help one to become a better person?

_____

_____

Vocabulary

Word List

HOSTLER	COACHMAN	GINGER
ACHE	BLACK	SIGN
HALTERS	HAND	SQUIRE
DIN	PRIDE	VIOLENT
BEAUTY	GEM	SPUR
GREEN	MANLY	RAVES
TWITCH	PINED	ROUSED
TOUR	MERRYLEGS	FLOG

Across

2. Employed to tend to horses
4. Spiked wheel on rider's boot
7. To beat
8. One who drives a carriage
11. Joe _____
12. Noise
13. Feeling of satisfaction
14. Smallish horse popular with the children of the novel
17. Jerking movement
19. Warlike
20. _____ Gordon
21. Wakened

Down

1. _____ Beauty
2. Straps used to lead horses
3. Omen
5. Longed for
6. Very sore
9. John _____
10. Black _____
11. Valuable stone
15. Brags loudly
16. Lively friend of Black Beauty
17. A guided journey
18. Unit used for measuring height of horses

NAME: _____

After You Read

Chapters Sixteen to Twenty

Part A

1. Complete the paragraphs with the correct words from the chapters.

The fire in the barn was probably caused by Towler's _____(a)____. Because he acted calm and cheery, _____(b)____ was able to lead the horses out of the fire. Shortly after Black Beauty was led from the blaze, the fire _____(c)____ arrived at the scene to put out the fire.

John was informed that Little Joe _____(d)____ was coming to replace James. He was coming for a try-out of _____(e)____ weeks. The horse that missed James the most when he left was _____(f)____.

One dark night Black Beauty was wakened by John, who was asked to fetch Doctor _____(g)____, because the _____(h)____ was deathly ill. From the barn to the doctor's was an _____(i)____-mile run. When Black Beauty returned from his run, Joe did not put a warm _____(j)____ on him because he thought Black Beauty would not like it. As a result, the horse almost _____(k)____. John was urged to forgive Joe, because what he did was out of _____(l)____.

2. Which answer best describes…

a) **John?**
- A wise
- B competent
- C noble
- D all of the above

b) **the response of the horses during the fire?**
- A didn't really care
- B panic
- C ignored the incident
- D tried to hide in their stalls

c) **John's reaction to Beauty's sickness?**
- A didn't care
- B anger and concern
- C furious with the Squire
- D thought it was silly

d) **Joe's reaction to the carter flogging the horses?**
- A didn't particularly care
- B found it amusing
- C wasn't his business
- D was angry

NAME: _____

Chapters Sixteen to Twenty

Part B

Answer the questions in complete sentences.

1. One of John Manly's rules was **"never to allow a pipe in the stable"**. Can you think of two additional rules that might make it safer for Black Beauty and the other horses?
   _____
   _____

2. One of the speakers in Chapter Sixteen says, **"Aye, he is a brave lad, and no mistake"**. Can you place the man's accent?
   _____
   _____

3. Why do you think **"it is one of the hardest things in the world to get horses out of a stable when there is either fire or flood"**?
   _____

4. James asks John what his thoughts are regarding the philosophy, **"Everybody look after himself, and take care of number one."** What are your thoughts about this expression? Do you agree or disagree? State your reasons.
   _____
   _____

5. What error in judgment did Joe make when tending to Black Beauty after his ride to fetch the doctor?
   _____
   _____

These chapters describe two very exciting adventures in Black Beauty's life. Two adventures, in fact, that almost cost him his life! Tell about a time in your own life when you experienced an adventure that proved to be life-threatening. If you can't think of such an experience, use your imagination!

NAME: _____

Chapters Twenty-one to Twenty-five

Answer the questions in complete sentences.

1. Have you ever moved to a different house or apartment? If so, describe what you found most difficult about the experience. If you haven't, imagine how difficult it might be.

   _____
   _____

2. What do you consider to be three important character traits in someone hired to work with horses (such as a hostler, groom, or driver)?

   _____
   _____

Vocabulary

Choose a word from the list that means the same or nearly the same as the underlined word.

| imperious | farrier | peculiar | obliged | vexed | chaise | amiable |

1. Joe put Merrylegs into the mistress' low **carriage** to take him to the vicarage.

2. The princess had the **odd** habit of coughing loudly before entering a room.

3. The teacher had a very **arrogant** manner in the classroom.

4. Master will be sorely **troubled**.

5. Black Beauty had a very **pleasant** disposition.

6. The **blacksmith** worked on Ginger's shoes for most of the morning.

7. She was **forced** to take far less than the vase was worth.

After You Read

Chapters Twenty-one to Twenty-five

Part A

Put a check mark next to the answer that is most correct.

1. **Merrylegs was sold to the Vicar under what condition?**
   - ○ A that he should never be sold
   - ○ B that the Squire be able to purchase him back at any time
   - ○ C that only children be allowed to ride him
   - ○ D that he be given his own stall and groom

2. **Which character in these chapters liked the use of the bearing rein?**
   - ○ A York
   - ○ B John
   - ○ C Lady W---
   - ○ D Mr. Gordon

3. **Which horse objected most strenuously to the bearing rein?**
   - ○ A Merrylegs
   - ○ B Black Beauty
   - ○ C Ginger
   - ○ D Max

4. **The people of which city were said to always want their horses to carry their heads high?**
   - ○ A New York
   - ○ B Liverpool
   - ○ C Paris
   - ○ D London

5. **Why did Lady Anne decide to ride Lizzie in Chapter Twenty-four?**
   - ○ A In size and appearance, Lizzie is far more a lady's horse.
   - ○ B Lady Anne's own horse, Black Beauty, was being shoed.
   - ○ C One of Lady Anne's sisters had suggested it to her.
   - ○ D Lady Anne was annoyed at her own horse, Black Beauty.

NAME: _____

After You Read

Chapters Twenty-one to Twenty-five

Part B

Answer the questions in complete sentences.

1. What crisis is described in Chapter Twenty-one?
   _____
   _____

2. Describe the character of Lady W---, from what we learn of her in this section.
   _____
   _____

3. What mistake in judgment did Lady Anne make in choosing her riding mount in Chapter Twenty-four?
   _____
   _____

4. This section describes two tumbles from a horse. Compare the similarities and differences of the two incidents.
   _____
   _____
   _____
   _____

5. Chapter Twenty-five ends in a type of cliffhanger. Reread the last paragraph and predict what you think might happen to Black Beauty and Smith.
   _____
   _____
   _____

One of the reasons that Anna Sewell wrote this novel was to bring to the attention of her readers the cruelties that many horses have to endure. Describe some of the ways that the horses in the novel have been mistreated. How might some of these particular cruelties have been prevented?

Before You Read

Chapters Twenty-six to Thirty

Answer the questions in complete sentences.

1. Think of at least two ways that a horse is at the mercy of its owner.

   _____

   _____

2. Can you think of any ways that society today can protect horses against being abused by cruel owners? (Be specific in your suggestions.)

   _____

   _____

Vocabulary

Choose a word from the list that means the same or nearly the same as the underlined word.

| slovenly | consequence | commotion | contempt | caustic | inquest | blemishes |

1. Forever after his accident Black Beauty carried the **scars** on his knees.

2. The **inquiry** revealed that Smith was at fault.

3. The acid was dangerous because it was so **corrosive**.

4. A tragic accident was the **result** of his carelessness.

5. He had a most **careless** appearance.

6. The players held a certain feeling of **disrespect** for that particular referee.

7. Ginger kicked up quite a **shindy** because of the bearing

NAME: _____

After You Read

Chapters Twenty-six to Thirty

Part A

1. Circle **T** if the statement is **TRUE** or **F** if it is **FALSE**.

    T F   a) The tumble that Black Beauty took because of Smith injured his knees.

    T F   b) Ginger exclaimed that she and Black Beauty were ruined by a drunkard and a fool.

    T F   c) The horse, Rory, was badly injured by a careless driver.

    T F   d) Peggy had an unusual gait because of her long legs.

    T F   e) Filcher was an honest groom who always made sure that Black Beauty was well fed and cared for.

    T F   f) A careless driver will often lead a horse into developing lazy habits.

2. Number the events from **1** to **6** in the order they occurred in the chapters.

    _____ a) Rory is badly injured in a road accident.

    _____ b) Black Beauty is cleared of all blame in Smith's death.

    _____ c) Black Beauty is sold to Mr. Barry.

    _____ d) Black Beauty is sold by the Earl to a livery stable.

    _____ e) Reuben Smith is killed and Black Beauty injured in an accident.

    _____ f) Black Beauty meets Ginger who tells him about being ruined by a foolish rider.

After You Read

NAME: _____

Chapters Twenty-six to Thirty

Part B

Answer the questions in complete sentences.

1. Look again at the five titles of these chapters. Which title do you find the most interesting? Explain the reason for your answer.
   _____
   _____

2. Give your personal impression of Reuben Smith. State one positive characteristic and one negative.
   _____
   _____

3. In the concluding paragraph of Chapter Twenty-six, Susan Smith asks the question, **"Why will they sell that cursed drink?"** How might you answer this difficult question?
   _____
   _____

4. Investigate: What is a job horse and what are his duties?
   _____
   _____
   _____

5. What is ironic about Filcher's name?
   _____
   _____

Journal Activity

In the novel we have been introduced to a number of characters that are cruel and uncaring when it comes to looking after a horse. Review the passage you have just read and describe in your journal your feelings about one of the uncaring people that passed through the life of Black Beauty or one of the other horses. Be sure to support your feelings with reasons why you feel as you do.

NAME: _____

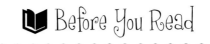

Chapters Thirty-one to Thirty-five

1. Under what circumstances would you say that a war is justified?
   _____
   _____
   _____

2. What character traits in an owner do you think would be important to a horse?
   _____
   _____
   _____

Vocabulary

Write a complete sentence using the following words from these chapters. (You may need to use a dictionary for some of the words.) Be sure to make the meaning of each word clear from its context.

1. **indolent** _____
2. **dejected** _____
3. **palisades** _____
4. **caparisoned** _____
5. **bayonet** _____
6. **restive** _____
7. **sham** _____
8. **portmanteau** _____

After You Read

Chapters Thirty-one to Thirty-five

Part A

1. Fill in each blank with the correct word from the chapters.

a) Alfred _____ was the laziest, most conceited fellow Black Beauty ever came near.

b) Black Beauty's groom was so lazy that the horse developed _____, a disease of the feet caused by foul stables.

c) Black Beauty was purchased by Jeremiah Barker at a horse _____.

d) Some of the other cab drivers thought Black Beauty would be especially good for a _____.

e) The Barker's other horse had once been an army horse who saw action in the _____ War.

f) The leader of the cab drivers was called Governor _____.

2. Use the words in the list to answer each question.

| Harry | Captain | Jack | Bayard | Mr. Barry | peace |

a) Captain's master during the war called him this.

b) Jerry said that Larry was always changing horses because he never gave them any of this.

c) This person was so disgusted at being twice deceived by his grooms that he decided to sell Black Beauty.

d) This person was the son of a cab driver.

e) The name given Black Beauty by the Barkers.

f) An older horse owned by the Barkers.

NAME: _____

After You Read

Chapters Thirty-one to Thirty-five

Part B

Answer the questions in complete sentences.

1. Anna Sewell's choice of names for her characters can be quite interesting. In Chapter Thirty-one we are introduced to Alfred Smirk. Do you think "Smirk" is a suitable name for this character? Defend your answer.

2. Black Beauty was a good and quick judge of character. Name two things about Jeremiah Barker that the horse immediately took to.

3. Do you think the following statement made by Captain is necessarily true: **"the enemy must have been awfully wicked people, if it was right to go all that way over the sea on purpose to kill them"**? Defend your answer.

4. Why do you think Jerry wouldn't take the extra half crown from the man for getting him to the station on time?

5. Decide whether the following statement is an example of **personification**, and then defend your answer: **"Good luck is rather particular who she rides with."**

 Imagine that you are Black Beauty and have just been sold to Jerry Barker. Describe your feelings about the man and your new home. Perhaps you can include detail not mentioned in the novel.

NAME: _____

Chapters Thirty-six to Forty

Answer the questions in complete sentences.

1. One of the characters in this section makes the comment about horses, **" 'Tis wonderful what they do understand"**. What do you think are the limits of a horse's understanding of our language?

   _____

   _____

2. What do we mean by "The Golden Rule"? Give your thoughts on this concept.

   _____

   _____

Vocabulary

Circle the word that matches the meaning of the underlined word in each sentence.

1. The elderly couple discovered a **foundling** at their front door in the morning.
   a) baby deer   b) abandoned infant   c) package of groceries   d) pet kitten

2. The can opener wasn't in a **convenient** location.
   a) topsy-turvy   b) old-fashioned   c) eager   d) handy

3. The street was often **thronged** with horses.
   a) punished   b) nearly empty   c) crowded   d) captured

4. My old grandmother was **oppressed** by the tsar of Russia.
   a) rewarded   b) introduced   c) knighted   d) persecuted

5. April's hair was very **lank** in appearance.
   a) dirty   b) dark and straight   c) long and lean   d) attractive

NAME: _____

Chapters Thirty-six to Forty

Part A

1. Complete the paragraphs with the correct words from the chapters.

Jerry refused to take a _____ -day license because it was too hard on
　　　　　　　　　　　　　　　　　a
him and too hard on his _____. Mr. Briggs asked Jerry about taking his wife to
　　　　　　　　　　　　　　b
_____ on Sunday mornings, but Jerry refused. Despite Jerry's strong beliefs in
　c
this matter, he agreed to drive Dinah _____ to her sick mother's on a Sunday.
　　　　　　　　　　　　　　　　　　　　　d
When he returned from his trip, he brought Dolly some _____.
　　　　　　　　　　　　　　　　　　　　　　　　　　　　　　　e

Seedy _____ was very upset because he had to pay too much for the
　　　　　f
rental of his _____. Often Sam had to work _____ hours a day, and still
　　　　　　　g　　　　　　　　　　　　　　　　　　h
had a difficult time making ends meet. He said that you must put your _____
　　　i
and children before the horse.

One day Black Beauty was surprised to meet his old friend, _____. How she
　　　　　　　　　　　　　　　　　　　　　　　　　　　　　　　　j
had changed! Her life was now full of _____. It was her wish that someone wou
　　　　　　　　　　　　　　　　　　　　　　k
ld _____ her before she came to such misery.
　　　l

2. Which answer best describes...

a) **Jerry?**
○ A   noble
○ B   bitter
○ C   sarcastic
○ D   rude

b) **Seedy Sam?**
○ A   humorous
○ B   up-beat
○ C   desperate
○ D   hopeful

c) **Ginger, in this section?**
○ A   downcast
○ B   up-beat
○ C   hopeful
○ D   self-fulfilled

d) **Skinner?**
○ A   thoughtful
○ B   considerate
○ C   greedy
○ D   talkative

After You Read

NAME: _____

Chapters Thirty-six to Forty

Part B

Answer the questions in complete sentences.

1. a) Why did Jerry take such a determined stand against driving his cab on Sundays?
   _____
   _____

   b) What was the one exception that he made to this rule? Why did he decide to make this particular exception?
   _____
   _____

2. Do you agree or disagree with the statement made to Jerry by the old gentleman: **"If we see cruelty or wrong that we have the power to stop, and do nothing, we make ourselves sharers in the guilt"**? Explain your answer.
   _____
   _____

3. a) Summarize the injustice that Seedy Sam was so upset about.
   _____
   _____

   b) What is meant by Sam's nickname, "Seedy"? Do you think this was a fair description of his character? Explain your answer.
   _____
   _____

Journal Activity: Imagine that you are one of Seedy Sam's children. Write a description of your situation and prospects following the sudden death of your father. Make sure that you include your innermost feelings regarding this unexpected development in your life.

NAME: _____

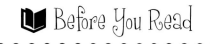 Before You Read

Chapters Forty-one to Forty-five

1. Chapter titles can often provide hints as to coming events in a novel. Take a look at the five chapter titles in this section. Choose one of the titles and predict what you think may happen in this particular chapter.
   _____
   _____

2. How would you describe the course of Black Beauty's life to this point? If you were Black Beauty, how might you be feeling?
   _____
   _____
   _____

Vocabulary

Circle the word that best matches the meaning of the underlined word in each sentence.

1. Harry referred to some of the boys in the neighborhood as **blackguards**.
   a) club members   b) boy scouts   c) soccer players   d) scoundrels

2. Dolly's **pinafore** was splattered with mud.
   a) stockings   b) dress   c) umbrella   d) hat

3. A **droll** smile came over Jerry's face.
   a) amused   b) unbelievable   c) picturesque   d) forced

4. The little girl had a large **blemish** on her forehead.
   a) scab   b) scar   c) flaw   d) scratch

5. "You'll never **repent** it," Jerry said to the Governor.
   a) borrow   b) buy   c) regret   d) leave

After You Read

NAME: _____

Chapters Forty-one to Forty-five

Part A

Put a check mark next to the answer that is most correct.

1. **Harry thrashed a group of boys for tormenting:**

    ○ **A** Molly
    ○ **B** Dolly
    ○ **C** Polly
    ○ **D** Harry

2. **Black Beauty and his master took the woman and her son to:**

    ○ **A** the market
    ○ **B** the hospital
    ○ **C** the boy's school
    ○ **D** her woman's parent's house

3. **Captain was replaced by:**

    ○ **A** Hotspur
    ○ **B** Challenger
    ○ **C** Dusty
    ○ **D** Horatio

4. **Jerry became very ill with what sickness?**

    ○ **A** pneumonia
    ○ **B** yellow fever
    ○ **C** tuberculosis
    ○ **D** bronchitis

5. **Jerry and his family were to go and work for:**

    ○ **A** Mrs. Fowler
    ○ **B** Captain Chelsey
    ○ **C** Professor Thoroughgood
    ○ **D** Inspector Grant

NAME: _____

After You Read

Chapters Forty-one to Forty-five

Part B

Answer the questions in complete sentences.

1. At the beginning of Chapter Forty-one Black Beauty sees a pony that reminds him of Merrylegs. What was one reason for Black Beauty believing it was not Merrylegs, and one reason why he thought it might be.

2. a) Investigate: In Chapter Forty-two, much is made of the colors of the different political parties. Even today in some countries, political parties are associated with specific colors. Research the political party of a country of your choice that is associated with a particular color. Give the name of the country, political party, and associated color.

   b) Jerry makes the statement: **"Liberty does not come from colors..."** In your own words, define the concept of liberty.

3. Why was Jerry so against the abuse of alcohol?

4. What does the following statement tell you about the character of one of Jerry's fares: **"as it is a card party, you may have to wait a few minutes, but don't be late"**?

Journal Activity

As this section draws to a close, Black Beauty once again faces the daunting task of changing owners. This must have been quite a frightening experience for him. In your journal entry imagine for a moment that you are Black Beauty and describe your feelings about going from Jerry's wonderful care – back into the unknown. What must Black Beauty have been thinking at this time?

Chapters Forty-six to Forty-nine

Answer the questions in complete sentences.

1. Describe how you would like to see the story of Black Beauty end.
   _____
   _____

2. What has the novel helped you to understand about the lives of horses, especially those that lived in the 1800's?
   _____
   _____

Vocabulary

With a straight line, connect each word on the left with its meaning on the right.

1	frequently	beg	A
2	persuasive	a tonic	B
3	fatigue	lasting	C
4	detain	dare	D
5	permanent	coax or tease	E
6	indignities	often	F
7	misery	unhappiness	G
8	beseech	enough	H
9	cordial	injuries	I
10	sufficient	tiredness	J
11	goad	delay, or keep from preceding	K
12	venture	convincing	L

NAME: _____

Chapters Forty-six to Forty-nine

Part A

1. Circle T if the statement is TRUE or F if it is FALSE.

T F a) Jakes, Black Beauty's carter, never used the bearing rein on his horses.

T F b) With Jakes as his carter, Black Beauty was often overloaded.

T F c) Nicholas Skinner, who came to own Black Beauty, was a different Skinner than the man who had been Seedy Sam's boss.

T F d) If Black Beauty had not been stolen from Skinner's stables by Joe Green, the horse would have been shot.

T F e) The kind farmer purchased Black Beauty at the sale for 50 pounds.

T F f) One of the ways that Joe Green recognized Black Beauty was from the white star on his forehead.

2. Number the events from 1 to 6 in the order they occurred in the chapters.

_____ a) Black Beauty is purchased by Mr. Thoroughgood.

_____ b) Black Beauty is reunited with Joe Green.

_____ c) Jerry sells Black Beauty to a corn dealer and baker.

_____ d) A woman intercedes for Black Beauty when he is being whipped.

_____ e) Black Beauty is sold to a large cab owner, Nicholas Skinner.

_____ f) Black Beauty collapses from exhaustion.

After You Read

Chapters Forty-six to Forty-nine

Part B

Answer the questions in complete sentences.

1. Do you agree or disagree with the following statement from Chapter Forty-Six: **"It is better to lead a good fashion than to follow a bad one."** Explain your answer.

2. Describe the character of Nicholas Skinner.

3. In Chapter Forty-eight, how did Grandpa know that there was a good deal of breeding about Black Beauty?

4. Again, Anna Sewell's choice of names for her characters is quite revealing. Why is this so about her choice of Mr. Thoroughgood's name?

5. The **climax** of the story usually occurs when the greatest problem or crisis of the novel is solved. Where would you say the climax of this novel occurs?

6. How was it **poetic justice** that Black Beauty end up back with Joe Green?

Were you pleased with the conclusion of the novel? Explain your feelings in this regard.

Writing Task #1

Chapters 1 to 8

Although the name of the area of England that Black Beauty is born in is not given, it is thought to be the same area that the author, Anna Sewell was from – Great Yarmouth, in Norfolk County. This was also the area that the great Charles Dickens set his novel, <u>David Copperfield</u>.

> **Your task is to <u>investigate the setting</u> of the novel, especially as it was in the mid 1800's.**
>
> Questions to consider: • What part of England was it in?
> • What was the countryside like? • What were the main towns of the area?
> • What were the main occupations of the population?
> • What were the main agricultural products, manufacturing products, etc.?
>
> Try to give the reader a vivid picture of what the home country of Black Beauty must have been like.

Chapters 9 to 16

> **Using your own artwork, photographs, or pictures cut from magazines, <u>create a scrapbook</u> illustrating Black Beauty's life to this point.**
>
> The scrapbook should contain titles, notes of explanation, and other memorabilia to help the reader get as clear a picture as possible of his life. You may also include in your scrapbook pictures of the people and other horses (or pictures that remind you of the people and horses) you have met by the end of Chapter Sixteen, and perhaps pictures of the places where Black Beauty lived.
>
> **Use your imagination and be creative!**
> When you are finished, your scrapbook should be a product that even Black Beauty would be proud to show to his mother!

Chapters 17 to 24

You are the editor of a small newspaper, The Derbyshire Free Press. The year is 1875, during the years that Anna Sewell was writing her classic novel. One afternoon Anna visits your office and most eloquently brings to your attention some of the great injustices that horses are forced to endure. She mentions such things as the cruelty of the bearing rein, blinkers and spurs, as well as several other matters of extreme cruelty that she has witnessed. By the time she leaves your newspaper office you are thoroughly convinced that her concerns are absolutely legitimate and you decide to write an editorial in the next issue of your newspaper bringing the matter before your readership.

> **Your task is to write an editorial of at least 150 words bringing Anna Sewell's concerns before the people of that day.**
>
> You may also wish to research this topic and add additional concerns as well. Remember, your task is to **convince** as many people as possible of the inhumane treatment that horses were being forced to endure.

Chapters 25 to 32

The story of Black Beauty has been made into a movie at least three times: in 1946, 1971, and 1994. As well, an updated version was released in 2005 called American Black Beauty, and was set in the United States. The novel was even made into a television series in 1972, The Adventures of Black Beauty.

> **Imagine that you have been hired to cast the stars for an updated version of the movie. Your responsibility is to cast actors for the following parts and briefly explain your choice:**
>
> - Farmer Grey • Squire Gordon • James Howard • John Manly
> - Joe Green • Colonel Blantyre • Lady W--- • Reuben Smith
>
> You may also wish to design a movie poster for your updated version, advertising the cast of stars that you have selected.

Writing Task #5

Chapters 33 to 40

You are the editor of a large magazine, <u>The London Bugle</u>, which is published in the area of England where Seedy Sam lived. You hear from one of Sam's friends about the cab driver's desperate last days and his death. You find yourself sickened by the circumstances leading to the poor man's death and the perilous circumstances that his family now find themselves in. You make arrangements to <u>interview</u> the man that Seedy Sam rented his horse and cab from – <u>Skinner</u>.

Prepare <u>at least five penetrating questions</u> to ask Skinner about his business and business practices to share with your readers.

Your questions should attempt to draw from this unscrupulous businessman his attitudes towards not only the horses in his stables, but other people as well.

Writing Task #6

Chapters 41 to 49

<u>Write a brief book review</u> of <u>Black Beauty</u> for posting on a website such as www.amazon.com.
Your review should be at least two paragraphs in length.

The first paragraph should briefly describe the plot (without giving away the ending).

The second paragraph should give the reviewer's impression of the novel. The reviewer should try to include one favorable comment and one suggestion as to how the novel might be improved.

NAME: _____

Word Search

Find all of the words in the Word Search. Words are written horizontally, vertically, diagonally, and some are even written backwards.

harness	refreshment	ignorance	feverish
frequently	stern	indolent	inquest
civil	liberty	oppressed	delicate
evidence	prompt	vice	blemish
consequence	animated	feeble	venture
disregard	constitution	injustice	canter
accommodation	passion	indignity	discontented

c	o	n	s	t	i	t	u	t	i	o	n	t	h	t	c	u	h
s	n	s	n	h	n	o	i	t	a	f	e	v	e	r	i	s	h
l	v	f	r	e	q	u	e	n	t	l	y	q	r	t	r	i	e
i	m	s	i	h	s	s	z	p	a	s	s	i	o	n	e	v	r
b	o	x	t	q	v	d	m	o	o	a	m	f	u	e	a	f	o
e	m	k	y	e	c	o	n	s	e	q	u	e	n	c	e	r	g
r	e	d	b	h	r	e	o	c	n	l	e	r	i	e	i	h	l
t	n	e	a	p	e	n	x	y	e	h	e	o	b	m	t	s	y
y	t	l	i	u	m	p	h	p	f	v	a	l	e	z	y	i	p
d	u	i	r	d	u	n	g	e	o	n	e	r	r	e	t	m	h
e	a	c	c	o	m	m	o	d	a	t	i	o	n	y	m	e	i
t	d	a	i	m	g	s	a	a	n	i	m	a	t	e	d	l	c
n	j	t	g	v	p	y	t	i	n	g	i	d	n	i	s	b	s
e	d	e	i	d	i	s	r	e	g	a	r	d	y	m	s	s	t
t	e	c	e	n	k	l	z	t	e	w	o	c	v	f	q	i	m
n	s	e	a	w	j	t	n	e	m	h	s	e	r	f	e	r	a
o	s	z	r	n	a	u	c	p	i	n	q	u	e	s	t	v	l
c	e	v	k	q	t	n	s	q	c	d	s	f	f	k	a	i	w
s	r	o	a	k	e	e	w	t	n	e	l	o	d	n	i	c	d
i	p	u	o	d	u	t	r	e	i	v	e	n	t	u	r	e	k
d	p	s	i	e	p	r	o	d	u	c	t	i	o	n	e	t	g
e	o	v	i	g	n	o	r	a	n	c	e	a	r	a	t	a	u
t	e	y	s	a	e	u	q	p	a	r	a	l	y	z	e	d	s

NAME: _____

After You Read

Comprehension Quiz

Answer the questions in complete sentences.

1. What were the names of two other horses that lived at Squire Gordon's with Black Beauty?
   _____
   _____

2. Why did Ginger have such an irritable disposition?
   _____
   _____

3. Describe why the bearing rein was so cruel a device.
   _____

4. Why were blinkers such a cruel device to use on horses?
   _____

5. Describe what happened to the horse, Captain, when he was in the Crimean War.
   _____
   _____

6. Why did Squire Gordon have to sell off Black Beauty and his other horses?
   _____
   _____

7. Who saved Black Beauty when the stable caught fire?
   _____

8. Describe how Joe Green almost killed Black Beauty "out of ignorance".
   _____
   _____

SUBTOTAL: ___/16

After You Read

NAME: _____

Comprehension Quiz

9. Describe Ginger's sad fate.
_____
_____

10. What was the one condition that the Squire gave the Vicar when he sold him Merrylegs?
_____
_____

11. Describe the circumstances leading up to Reuben Smith's death.
_____
_____

12. How did Seedy Sam find himself in such a desperate situation?
_____
_____

13. Describe how Jerry Barker made his living.
_____
_____

14. Why did Jerry not take out a seven-day license? (Try to think of two reasons.)
_____
_____

15. Who did Black Beauty end up back with at the end of the novel?
_____
_____

SUBTOTAL: /14

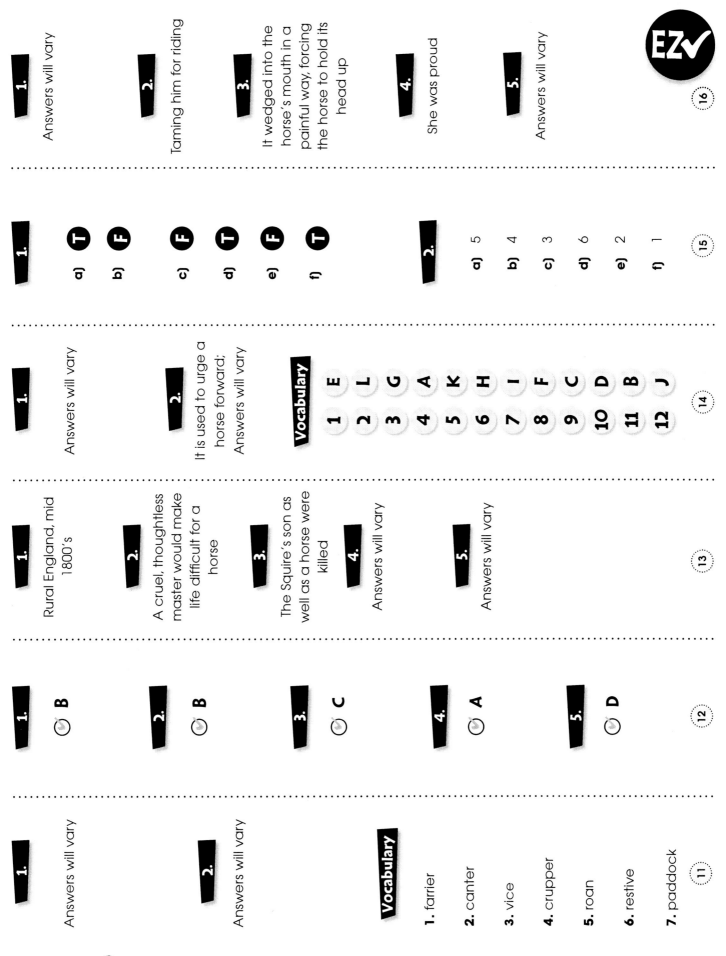

EZ ✓

1. Answers will vary

2. Probably Scottish

3. Answers will vary

4. Answers will vary

5. He didn't put a blanket over him

1.
- a) pipe
- b) James
- c) engine
- d) Green
- e) six
- f) Merrylegs
- g) White
- h) mistress
- i) eight
- j) cloth
- k) died
- l) ignorance

2.
- a) ⊙ D
- b) ⊙ B
- c) ⊙ B
- d) ⊙ D

---

1. Answers will vary

Vocabulary

Across:
2. hostler
4. spur
7. flog
8. coachman
11. Green
12. din
13. pride
14. Merrylegs
17. twitch
19. violent
20. Squire
21. roused

Down:
1. Black
2. halters
3. sign
5. pined
6. ache
9. Manly
10. Beauty
11. gem
15. raves
16. Ginger
17. tour
18. hand

---

1. It's not worth dieing over a sport like fox-hunting

2. He had a kind heart and liked and respected his animals

3. It would worry and fatigue the horse and decrease its strength

4. Answers will vary

5. Answers will vary (i.e. if you don't control your emotions, you will hurt yourself and others)

1.
- a) Sawyer
- b) bridge
- c) farmers'
- d) cruelty
- e) James Howard
- f) Gordon

2.
- a) Grey
- b) Langley
- c) John
- d) Bushby
- e) James

---

1. Answers will vary

2. Answers will vary

Vocabulary

1. oppressed
2. wrenched
3. fatigued
4. chaise
5. droll
6. livery
7. hostler

EZ ✓

Page 23

1. Answers will vary
2. Answers will vary

Vocabulary
1. chaise
2. peculiar
3. imperious
4. vexed
5. amiable
6. farrier
7. obliged

Page 24

1. A
2. C
3. C
4. D
5. A

Page 25

1. The Squire's family was moving and sold all their horses
2. She was proud and concerned about appearances
3. Ginger was too frisky
4. Lady Anne was thrown from Lizzie when the mare was frightened; Smith fell from Black Beauty after he drove the horse too hard with a broken shoe
5. Answers will vary

Page 26

1. Answers will vary
2. Answers will vary

Vocabulary
1. blemishes
2. inquest
3. caustic
4. consequence
5. slovenly
6. contempt
7. commotion

Page 27

1.
   a) T
   b) T
   c) T
   d) F
   e) F
   f) T

2.
   a) 5
   b) 2
   c) 6
   d) 4
   e) 1
   f) 3

Page 28

1. Answers will vary
2. Answers will vary (i.e. gentle and clever; an alcoholic)
3. Answers will vary
4. A horse that's hired out by its owner
5. "Filch" means to steal something

EZ ✓

1.
a) Answers will vary (i.e. to protect his horses, himself; to be with family)

b) Dinah; Answers will vary

2. Answers will vary

3.
a) He was charged so much to rent his horses and cab, he could not support his family

b) "Seedy" means shabby or dishonest; Answers will vary

1.
a) seven
b) horses
c) church
d) Brown
e) flowers
f) Sam
g) cab and horses
h) 14 to 16
i) wife
j) Ginger
k) misery
l) shoot

2.
a) ○ A b) ● C
c) ● A d) ○ C

---

1. Answers will vary

2. Answers will vary

Vocabulary

1. b
2. d
3. c
4. d
5. c

---

1. Answers will vary

2. He spoke kindly; he had a kindly, cheery look

3. Answers will vary

4. Answers will vary (i.e. he was just doing his job)

5. "Luck" is being personified

1.
a) Smirk
b) thrush
c) fair
d) funeral
e) Crimean
f) Grant

2.
a) Bayard
b) peace
c) Mr. Barry
d) Harry
e) Jack
f) Captain

---

1. Answers will vary

2. Answers will vary

Vocabulary

Answers will vary (the meaning of each word should be clearly conveyed in its sentence)

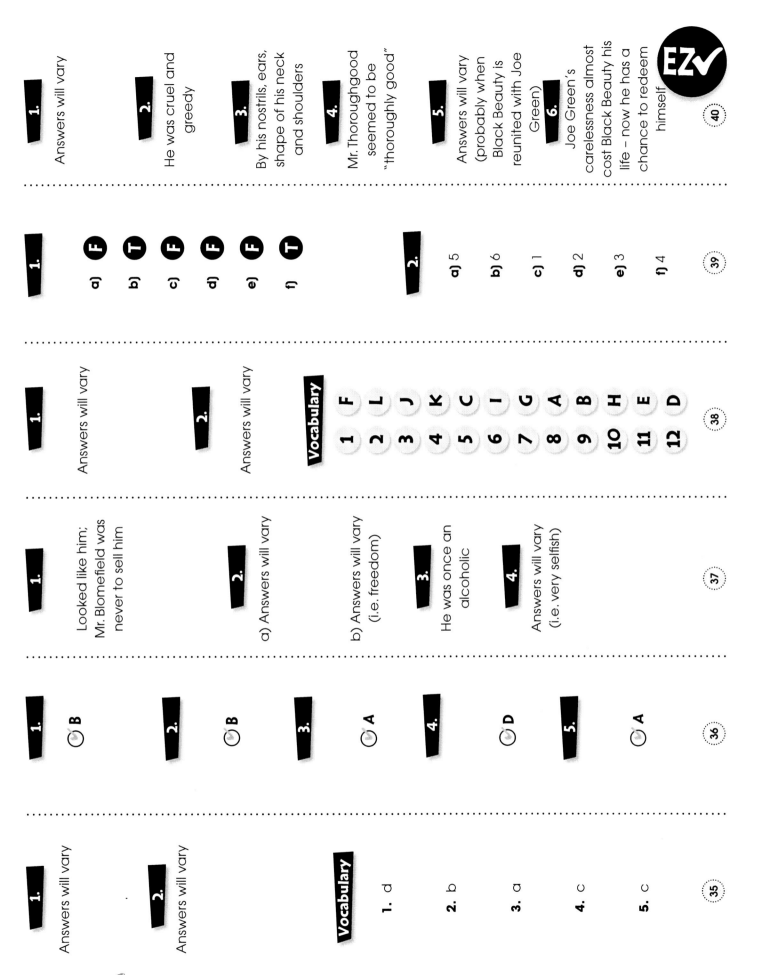

Word Search Answers

1. Ginger and Merrylegs
2. She had had a cruel master
3. It forced the horse's head up so that it was much harder to pull a cart or wagon
4. Blinkers were dangerous, as they impaired a horse's vision
5. His master had been killed in a battle
6. His wife became ill and they had to move
7. James Howard
8. Joe did not cover Black Beauty with a blanket after the horse had been ridden very hard
9. She fell into the hands of a cruel master and was worked to death
10. That the horse must never be sold
11. When drunk he rode Black Beauty very hard. The horse lost a shoe and stumbled, killing Smith.
12. Sam had to pay such high rent for his cab and horses, he couldn't support his family
13. He drove a cab
14. Too hard on him and his horses; He wanted to spend time with his family
15. Joe Green

Owners, Owners Everywhere

Who were the ten people that owned Black Beauty over the course of his lifetime? Record the names of his owners and grooms (if given), and whether the owner was good, bad or so-so. Make sure your list is in correct chronological order.

	OWNER	GROOM	GOOD, BAD OR SO-SO?
1			
2			
3			
4			
5			
6			
7			
8			
9			
10			

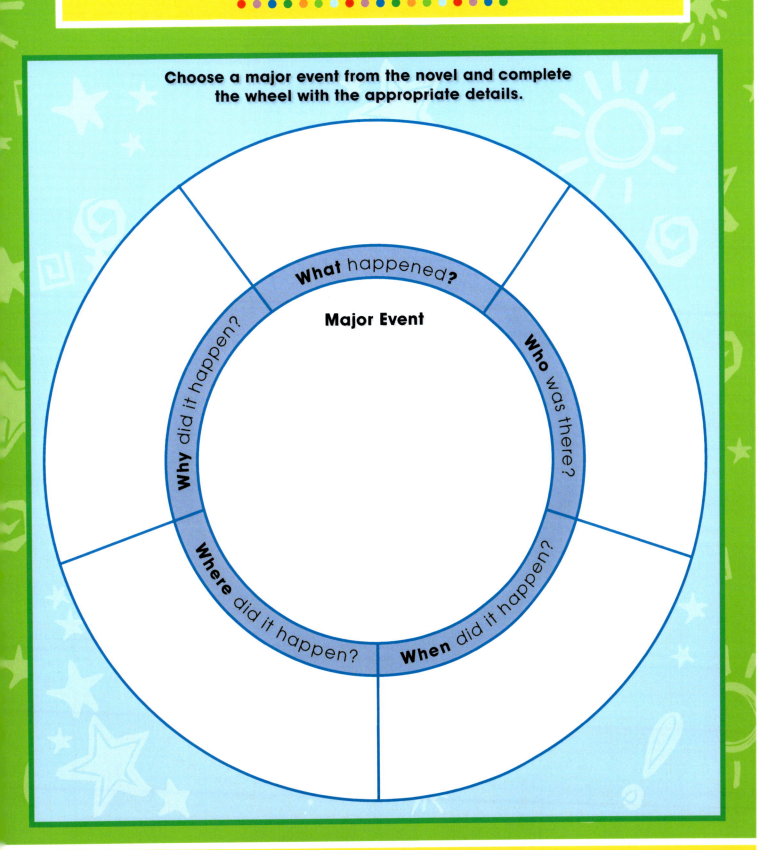

Compare and Contrast Matrix

Compare and contrast two characters from the novel. Choose either **TWO PEOPLE** or **TWO HORSES**.

Physical and Characters Attributes for Comparison	Character 1	Character 2
1 Physical or Character Attribute?		
2 Physical or Character Attribute?		
3 Physical or Character Attribute?		

Publication Listing

Ask Your Dealer About Our Complete Line

SOCIAL STUDIES - Books

ITEM #	TITLE
	DAILY LIFE SKILLS SERIES
CC5790	Daily Marketplace Skills
CC5791	Daily Social & Workplace Skills
CC5792	Daily Health & Hygiene Skills
CC5793	Daily Life Skills Big Book
	MAPPING SKILLS SERIES
CC5786	Grades PK-2 Mapping Skills with Google Earth
CC5787	Grades 3-5 Mapping Skills with Google Earth
CC5788	Grades 6-8 Mapping Skills with Google Earth
CC5789	Grades PK-8 Mapping Skills with Google Earth Big Book
	NORTH AMERICAN GOVERNMENTS SERIES
CC5757	American Government
CC5758	Canadian Government
CC5759	Mexican Government
CC5760	Governments of North America Big Book
	WORLD GOVERNMENTS SERIES
CC5761	World Political Leaders
CC5762	World Electoral Processes
CC5763	Capitalism vs. Communism
CC5777	World Politics Big Book
	WORLD CONFLICT SERIES
CC5511	American Revolutionary War
CC5500	American Civil War
CC5512	American Wars Big Book
CC5501	World War I
CC5502	World War II
CC5503	World Wars I & II Big Book
CC5505	Korean War
CC5506	Vietnam War
CC5507	Korean & Vietnam Wars Big Book
CC5508	Persian Gulf War (1990-1991)
CC5509	Iraq War (2003-2010)
CC5510	Gulf Wars Big Book
	WORLD CONTINENTS SERIES
CC5750	North America
CC5751	South America
CC5768	The Americas Big Book
CC5752	Europe
CC5753	Africa
CC5754	Asia
CC5755	Australia
CC5756	Antarctica
	WORLD CONNECTIONS SERIES
CC5782	Culture, Society & Globalization
CC5783	Economy & Globalization
CC5784	Technology & Globalization
CC5785	Globalization Big Book

REGULAR & REMEDIAL EDUCATION

Reading Level 3-4 Grades 5-8

SOCIAL STUDIES - Software

ITEM #	TITLE
	MAPPING SKILLS SERIES
CC7770	Grades PK-2 Mapping Skills with Google Earth
CC7771	Grades 3-5 Mapping Skills with Google Earth
CC7772	Grades 6-8 Mapping Skills with Google Earth
CC7773	Grades PK-8 Mapping Skills with Google Earth Big Box

SCIENCE - Software

	SPACE AND BEYOND SERIES
CC7557	Solar System Grades 5-8
CC7558	Galaxies & the Universe Grades 5-8
CC7559	Space Travel & Technology Grades 5-8
CC7560	Space Big Box Grades 5-8
	HUMAN BODY SERIES
CC7549	Cells, Skeletal & Muscular Systems Grades 5-8
CC7550	Senses, Nervous & Respiratory Systems Grades 5-8
CC7551	Circulatory, Digestive & Reproductive Systems Grades 5-8
CC7552	Human Body Big Box Grades 5-8
	FORCE, MOTION & SIMPLE MACHINES SERIES
CC7553	Force Grades 3-8
CC7554	Motion Grades 3-8
CC7555	Simple Machines Grades 3-8
CC7556	Force, Motion & Simple Machines Big Box Grades 3-8

ENVIRONMENTAL STUDIES - Software

	CLIMATE CHANGE SERIES
CC7747	Global Warming: Causes Grades 3-8
CC7748	Global Warming: Effects Grades 3-8
CC7749	Global Warming: Reduction Grades 3-8
CC7750	Global Warming Big Box Grades 3-8

LANGUAGE ARTS - Software

CC7112	Word Families - Short Vowels Grades PK-2
CC7113	Word Families - Long Vowels Grades PK-2
CC7114	Word Families - Vowels Big Box Grades PK-2
CC7100	High Frequency Sight Words Grades PK-2
CC7101	High Frequency Picture Words Grades PK-2
CC7102	Sight & Picture Words Big Box Grades PK-2
CC7104	How to Write a Paragraph Grades 3-8
CC7105	How to Write a Book Report Grades 3-8
CC7106	How to Write an Essay Grades 3-8
CC7107	Master Writing Big Box Grades 3-8
CC7108	Reading Comprehension Grades 5-8
CC7109	Literary Devices Grades 5-8
CC7110	Critical Thinking Grades 5-8
CC7111	Master Reading Big Box Grades 5-8

SCIENCE - Books

ITEM #	TITLE
	ECOLOGY & THE ENVIRONMENT SERIES
CC4500	Ecosystems
CC4501	Classification & Adaptation
CC4502	Cells
CC4503	Ecology & The Environment Big Book
	MATTER & ENERGY SERIES
CC4504	Properties of Matter
CC4505	Atoms, Molecules & Elements
CC4506	Energy
CC4507	The Nature of Matter Big Book
	FORCE & MOTION SERIES
CC4508	Force
CC4509	Motion
CC4510	Simple Machines
CC4511	Force, Motion & Simple Machines Big Book
	SPACE & BEYOND SERIES
CC4512	Solar System
CC4513	Galaxies & The Universe
CC4514	Travel & Technology
CC4515	Space Big Book
	HUMAN BODY SERIES
CC4516	Cells, Skeletal & Muscular Systems
CC4517	Senses, Nervous & Respiratory Systems
CC4518	Circulatory, Digestive & Reproductive Systems
CC4519	Human Body Big Book

ENVIRONMENTAL STUDIES - Books

	MANAGING OUR WASTE SERIES
CC5764	Waste: At the Source
CC5765	Prevention, Recycling & Conservation
CC5766	Waste: The Global View
CC5767	Waste Management Big Book
	CLIMATE CHANGE SERIES
CC5769	Global Warming: Causes
CC5770	Global Warming: Effects
CC5771	Global Warming: Reduction
CC5772	Global Warming Big Book
	GLOBAL WATER SERIES
CC5773	Conservation: Fresh Water Resources
CC5774	Conservation: Ocean Water Resources
CC5775	Conservation: Waterway Habitat Resources
CC5776	Water Conservation Big Book
	CARBON FOOTPRINT SERIES
CC5778	Reducing Your Own Carbon Footprint
CC5779	Reducing Your School's Carbon Footprint
CC5780	Reducing Your Community's Carbon Footprint
CC5781	Carbon Footprint Big Book

VISIT:
www.CLASSROOMCOMPLETEPRESS.com
To view sample pages from each book

LITERATURE KITS™ - Books

GRADES 1-2

ITEM #	TITLE
CC2100	Curious George (H. A. Rey)
CC2101	Paper Bag Princess (Robert N. Munsch)
CC2102	Stone Soup (Marcia Brown)
CC2103	The Very Hungry Caterpillar (Eric Carle)
CC2104	Where the Wild Things Are (Maurice Sendak)

GRADES 3-4

ITEM #	TITLE
CC2300	Babe: The Gallant Pig (Dick King-Smith)
CC2301	Because of Winn-Dixie (Kate DiCamillo)
CC2302	The Tale of Despereaux (Kate DiCamillo)
CC2303	James and the Giant Peach (Roald Dahl)
CC2304	Ramona Quimby, Age 8 (Beverly Cleary)
CC2305	The Mouse and the Motorcycle (Beverly Cleary)
CC2306	Charlotte's Web (E.B. White)
CC2307	Owls in the Family (Farley Mowat)
CC2308	Sarah, Plain and Tall (Patricia MacLachlan)
CC2309	Matilda (Roald Dahl)
CC2310	Charlie & The Chocolate Factory (Roald Dahl)
CC2311	Frindle (Andrew Clements)
CC2312	M.C. Higgins, the Great (Virginia Hamilton)
CC2313	The Family Under The Bridge (N.S. Carlson)
CC2314	The Hundred Penny Box (Sharon Mathis)
CC2315	Cricket in Times Square (George Selden)
CC2316	Fantastic Mr Fox (Roald Dahl)
CC2317	The Hundred Dresses (Eleanor Estes)
CC2318	The War with Grandpa (Robert Kimmel Smith)

GRADES 5-6

ITEM #	TITLE
CC2500	Black Beauty (Anna Sewell)
CC2501	Bridge to Terabithia (Katherine Paterson)
CC2502	Bud, Not Buddy (Christopher Paul Curtis)
CC2503	The Egypt Game (Zilpha Keatley Snyder)
CC2504	The Great Gilly Hopkins (Katherine Paterson)
CC2505	Holes (Louis Sachar)
CC2506	Number the Stars (Lois Lowry)
CC2507	The Sign of the Beaver (E.G. Speare)
CC2508	The Whipping Boy (Sid Fleischman)
CC2509	Island of the Blue Dolphins (Scott O'Dell)
CC2510	Underground to Canada (Barbara Smucker)
CC2511	Loser (Jerry Spinelli)
CC2512	The Higher Power of Lucky (Susan Patron)
CC2513	Kira-Kira (Cynthia Kadohata)
CC2514	Dear Mr. Henshaw (Beverly Cleary)
CC2515	The Summer of the Swans (Betsy Byars)
CC2516	Shiloh (Phyllis Reynolds Naylor)
CC2517	A Single Shard (Linda Sue Park)
CC2518	Hoot (Carl Hiaasen)
CC2519	Hatchet (Gary Paulsen)
CC2520	The Giver (Lois Lowry)
CC2521	The Graveyard Book (Neil Gaiman)
CC2522	The View From Saturday (E.L. Konigsburg)
CC2523	Hattie Big Sky (Kirby Larson)
CC2524	When You Reach Me (Rebecca Stead)
CC2525	Criss Cross (Lynne Rae Perkins)
CC2526	A Year Down Yonder (Richard Peck)
CC2527	Maniac Magee (Jerry Spinelli)

LITERATURE KITS™ - Books

ITEM #	TITLE
CC2528	From the Mixed-Up Files of Mrs. Basil E. Frankweiler (E.L. Konigsburg)
CC2529	Sing Down the Moon (Scott O'Dell)
CC2530	The Phantom Tollbooth (Norton Juster)
CC2531	Gregor the Overlander (Suzanne Collins)

GRADES 7-8

ITEM #	TITLE
CC2700	Cheaper by the Dozen (Frank B. Gilbreth)
CC2701	The Miracle Worker (William Gibson)
CC2702	The Red Pony (John Steinbeck)
CC2703	Treasure Island (Robert Louis Stevenson)
CC2704	Romeo & Juliet (William Shakespeare)
CC2705	Crispin: The Cross of Lead (Avi)
CC2706	Call It Courage (Armstrong Sperry)
CC2707	The Boy in the Striped Pajamas (John Boyne)
CC2708	The Westing Game (Ellen Raskin)
CC2709	The Cay (Theodore Taylor)
CC2710	The Hunger Games (Suzanne Collins)

GRADES 9-12

ITEM #	TITLE
CC2001	To Kill A Mockingbird (Harper Lee)
CC2002	Angela's Ashes (Frank McCourt)
CC2003	The Grapes of Wrath (John Steinbeck)
CC2004	The Good Earth (Pearl S. Buck)
CC2005	The Road (Cormac McCarthy)
CC2006	The Old Man and the Sea (Ernest Hemingway)
CC2007	Lord of the Flies (William Golding)
CC2008	The Color Purple (Alice Walker)
CC2009	The Outsiders (S.E. Hinton)
CC2010	Hamlet (William Shakespeare)
CC2011	The Great Gatsby (F. Scott Fitzgerald)
CC2012	The Adventures of Huckleberry Finn (Mark Twain)
CC2013	Macbeth (William Shakespeare)
CC2014	Fahrenheit 451 (Ray Bradbury)

LANGUAGE ARTS - Books

ITEM #	TITLE
CC1110	Word Families - Short Vowels Grades K-1
CC1111	Word Families - Long Vowels Grades K-1
CC1112	Word Families - Vowels Big Book Grades K-1
CC1113	High Frequency Sight Words Grades K-1
CC1114	High Frequency Picture Words Grades K-1
CC1115	Sight & Picture Words Big Book Grades K-1
CC1100	How to Write a Paragraph Grades 5-8
CC1101	How to Write a Book Report Grades 5-8
CC1102	How to Write an Essay Grades 5-8
CC1103	Master Writing Big Book Grades 5-8
CC1116	Reading Comprehension Grades 5-8
CC1117	Literary Devices Grades 5-8
CC1118	Critical Thinking Grades 5-8
CC1119	Master Reading Big Book Grades 5-8
CC1106	Reading Response Forms: Grades 1-2
CC1107	Reading Response Forms: Grades 3-4
CC1108	Reading Response Forms: Grades 5-6
CC1109	Reading Response Forms Big Book: Grades 1-6

MATHEMATICS - Software

ITEM #	TITLE
	PRINCIPLES & STANDARDS OF MATH SERIES
CC7315	Grades PK-2 Five Strands of Math Big Box
CC7316	Grades 3-5 Five Strands of Math Big Box
CC7317	Grades 6-8 Five Strands of Math Big Box

MATHEMATICS - Books

TASK SHEETS

ITEM #	TITLE
CC3100	Grades PK-2 Number & Operations Task Sheets
CC3101	Grades PK-2 Algebra Task Sheets
CC3102	Grades PK-2 Geometry Task Sheets
CC3103	Grades PK-2 Measurement Task Sheets
CC3104	Grades PK-2 Data Analysis & Probability Task Sheets
CC3105	Grades PK-2 Five Strands of Math Big Book Task Sheets
CC3106	Grades 3-5 Number & Operations Task Sheets
CC3107	Grades 3-5 Algebra Task Sheets
CC3108	Grades 3-5 Geometry Task Sheets
CC3109	Grades 3-5 Measurement Task Sheets
CC3110	Grades 3-5 Data Analysis & Probability Task Sheets
CC3111	Grades 3-5 Five Strands of Math Big Book Task Sheets
CC3112	Grades 6-8 Number & Operations Task Sheets
CC3113	Grades 6-8 Algebra Task Sheets
CC3114	Grades 6-8 Geometry Task Sheets
CC3115	Grades 6-8 Measurement Task Sheets
CC3116	Grades 6-8 Data Analysis & Probability Task Sheets
CC3117	Grades 6-8 Five Strands of Math Big Book Task Sheets

DRILL SHEETS

ITEM #	TITLE
CC3200	Grades PK-2 Number & Operations Drill Sheets
CC3201	Grades PK-2 Algebra Drill Sheets
CC3202	Grades PK-2 Geometry Drill Sheets
CC3203	Grades PK-2 Measurement Drill Sheets
CC3204	Grades PK-2 Data Analysis & Probability Drill Sheets
CC3205	Grades PK-2 Five Strands of Math Big Book Drill Sheets
CC3206	Grades 3-5 Number & Operations Drill Sheets
CC3207	Grades 3-5 Algebra Drill Sheets
CC3208	Grades 3-5 Geometry Drill Sheets
CC3209	Grades 3-5 Measurement Drill Sheets
CC3210	Grades 3-5 Data Analysis & Probability Drill Sheets
CC3211	Grades 3-5 Five Strands of Math Big Book Drill Sheets
CC3212	Grades 6-8 Number & Operations Drill Sheets
CC3213	Grades 6-8 Algebra Drill Sheets
CC3214	Grades 6-8 Geometry Drill Sheets
CC3215	Grades 6-8 Measurement Drill Sheets
CC3216	Grades 6-8 Data Analysis & Probability Drill Sheets
CC3217	Grades 6-8 Five Strands of Math Big Book Drill Sheets

TASK & DRILL SHEETS

ITEM #	TITLE
CC3300	Grades PK-2 Number & Operations Task & Drill Sheets
CC3301	Grades PK-2 Algebra Task & Drill Sheets
CC3302	Grades PK-2 Geometry Task & Drill Sheets
CC3303	Grades PK-2 Measurement Task & Drill Sheets
CC3304	Grades PK-2 Data Analysis & Probability Task & Drills
CC3306	Grades 3-5 Number & Operations Task & Drill Sheets
CC3307	Grades 3-5 Algebra Task & Drill Sheets
CC3308	Grades 3-5 Geometry Task & Drill Sheets
CC3309	Grades 3-5 Measurement Task & Drill Sheets
CC3310	Grades 3-5 Data Analysis & Probability Task & Drills
CC3312	Grades 6-8 Number & Operations Task & Drill Sheets
CC3313	Grades 6-8 Algebra Task & Drill Sheets
CC3314	Grades 6-8 Geometry Task & Drill Sheets
CC3315	Grades 6-8 Measurement Task & Drill Sheets
CC3316	Grades 6-8 Data Analysis & Probability Task & Drills

www.CLASSROOM COMPLETE PRESS.com

A *Literature Kit*™ FOR

Black Beauty

By Anna Sewell

Written by Nat Reed

GRADES 5 – 6

Classroom Complete Press
P.O. Box 19729
San Diego, CA 92159
Tel: 1-800-663-3609 / Fax: 1-800-663-3608
Email: service@classroomcompletepress.com

www.classroomcompletepress.com

ISBN-13: 978-1-55319-332-6
ISBN-10: 1-55319-332-6

© 2006

Permission to Reproduce

Permission is granted to the individual teacher who purchases one copy of this book to reproduce the student activity material for use in his or her classroom only. Reproduction of these materials for colleagues, an entire school or school system, or for commercial sale is strictly prohibited. No part of this publication may be transmitted in any form or by any means, electronic, mechanical, recording or otherwise without the prior written permission of the publisher. We acknowledge the financial support of the Government of Canada through the Book Publishing Industry Development Program (BPIDP) for our publishing activities. Printed in Canada. All rights reserved.

Critical Thinking Skills

Black Beauty

Skills For Critical Thinking		1-5	6-10	11-15	16-20	21-25	26-30	31-35	36-40	41-45	46-49	Writing Tasks	Graphic Organizers
LEVEL 1 Knowledge	• Identify Story Elements	✓	✓	✓	✓	✓	✓	✓	✓	✓	✓	✓	✓
	• Recall Details	✓	✓	✓	✓	✓	✓	✓	✓	✓	✓	✓	✓
	• Match	✓	✓	✓		✓	✓	✓	✓	✓	✓	✓	✓
	• Sequence			✓			✓				✓		✓
LEVEL 2 Comprehension	• Compare Characters	✓	✓			✓	✓		✓			✓	✓
	• Summarize	✓	✓	✓		✓	✓	✓	✓		✓	✓	✓
	• State Main Idea			✓					✓	✓			
	• Describe	✓	✓	✓		✓	✓	✓	✓	✓		✓	✓
	• Classify			✓			✓		✓				
LEVEL 3 Application	• Plan	✓		✓				✓				✓	✓
	• Interview											✓	
	• Infer Outcomes	✓	✓	✓	✓			✓					
LEVEL 4 Analysis	• Draw Conclusions	✓	✓	✓	✓	✓	✓	✓	✓	✓		✓	✓
	• Identify Supporting Evidence	✓	✓	✓		✓	✓		✓	✓	✓	✓	✓
	• Infer Motivations	✓	✓	✓	✓			✓					
	• Identify Cause & Effect	✓	✓	✓	✓	✓							
LEVEL 5 Synthesis	• Predict	✓		✓	✓	✓	✓	✓	✓				
	• Design											✓	
	• Create	✓		✓		✓		✓	✓			✓	
	• Imagine Alternatives									✓	✓		
LEVEL 6 Evaluation	• Defend An Opinion	✓	✓	✓	✓	✓	✓	✓	✓	✓	✓	✓	✓
	• Make Judgements	✓	✓	✓	✓	✓	✓	✓	✓	✓	✓	✓	✓

Based on Bloom's Taxonomy